stoopid

Poems

edward walker

This was the life for a man, to wander and stop and
then go on, ever following the white line along
the rambling coast, a time to relax at the wheel,
light another cigarette, and grope stupidly for
the meanings in that perplexing desert sky.

—John Fante

"And so I go to the woods. As I go in under the trees,
dependably, almost at once, and by nothing I do, things
fall into place. I enter an order that does not exist
outside, in the human spaces....I am less important
than I thought. I rejoice in that."

—Wendell Berry

Appeared in Poetry collection Turtle Crossing: *Adhan, The Gift, Reflections, Dawning, Grown Up, New Day, Grand Canyon, Growing by Half.*

Paperback: ISBN 979-8-218-38392-3

Text font ITC Baskerville

Table of Contents

Preface

This collection of poems begins in Brooklyn, NY in the 1950s and continues through the decades to present. It is autobiographic and many of the poems are memoirs. They are a record of the winding roads I travelled to arrive here in Guilford, CT and Amagansett, NY, with a nod to good friends along the way.

—edward walker
Guilford, CT
2024

63rd Street

In a two-story four-family walkup
grandma Lena owned but lived across the street
with her second husband insurance broker.
Aunt Etta and uncle Ben lived downstairs.
Ben, ten years older than his brother
my father, Etta, a Christian scientist.
Uncle Irving and aunt Sophie, father's sister,
lived in the apartment across the hall
that we broke through to cousin Peter's room
adding a bedroom to our apartment
for my sister and I when Peter eloped
and the family went Yiddish.
My parents begot a bedroom, no longer sleeping
on a living room pullout. The fourth apartment rented
to a doughnut baker, paid our bills.

—October 1958 journal entry;
family trip
eight years old
drove through Amish country
walked through Williamsburg
stuck in stocks
drove Skyline Drive
White House—

(continued)

The same year aunt Etta yelled at me
for shooting caps on the stoop. Later that day
cousins' Mel and Norman shot caps on the same stoop
into the smiling eyes of their sweet grandmother Etta
before she tripped over a telephone cord,
the long ones that were in every home,
and broke her shoulder and wouldn't take aspirin.

I cried laying in a carriage on the
Coney Island boardwalk during July-fourth fireworks.
At two I split my forehead open
playing peek-a-boo at gramps's house.
A doctor stapled my head.
I played stoopball for hours, threw Spaldings
in a narrow alley with trash cans
hard against the opposite wall
catching it like Mickey Mantle,
Yogi Berra, Willie Mays.
Grew tomatoes and cucumbers
in our rear rocky garden shaded
by six-floor apartment buildings
filled with policemen and garbagemen,
curlers and kids. Our side neighbor Italy
grew a colorful garden filled with many vegetables.
We peed arcs between Chevy fins and Ford grills,
spit seven boxes, grew older and dumber
wild in streets. Mouse flung flattened cans
and boxes like discus—broken window runs—
Sal threw Howie, Temma's brother
through a plate-glass window on Bay Parkway
—amazing grace

Sal smashed a ceiling lightbulb with his head
cool-jumping a chair at a basement party.
We laughed like there was no tomorrow.
We pulled fuses out of fire-crackers and
emptied the powder then twisted their tails
creating a 'slow-fuse' that we pushed
into piles of shit by the curb
waiting for anybody to walk by. I remember
a tall man in a tan coat splattered
in all good fun for us scurrying between
parked cars city rats that we were
climbing elms like nuts throwing itchy-balls
before Dutch elm disease, before puberty
before the N train left the station.

Family Cruise

My parents took my sister and I
to see my aunt and uncle off
on a cruise ship only they could afford

On ship, the music in the glittered ballroom
attracted me like gravity to horns on
the bandstand. I sat mesmerized
until last call crackled us poor non-passengers
to disembark onto city streets
where we found our car and drove
into a westside sea of traffic
in our boat of a hand me down Ford
with Sinatra singing us down river

Adhan

I'm tossing letters like salad
flipping from bottom to top
then tilling in compost
until one day water
germinating seeds reminding me

I too was young
without sense of time
tugging my comings and goings
except for ma's dinner-chant yell
shouted over elms on 63rd street

In winter, when dusk fell early
and my fingers and toes numb with cold
I welcomed that yell like a call to prayer,
and with my wool hat and gloves thrown
onto the radiator I ran past
through hallway smells
soothing my soul to believing
this would be forever

All Fall Down

I lift my mother off the floor
fussing with balance
to lean her against her walker
relieved
both of us I guess
pleased she can still walk
surprised I forgot how
really heavy she could be

Out the nursing home window
a heron on one leg laughs
and I feel new cells grow
with each visit, then shed
all over the past, driving
the dark road home

For Frances

Mom died nine years ago,
cemetery behind I paid bills,
left the rest with my sister.
tonight we watch home movies,
mom waves, our black lab,
buried in woods out back,
wags her tail

Months later, night driving
on crushed black snow
Garrison Keillor read a poem
and his soothing voice settled me
and when he finished a dirge played
and never hearing one before
I sped past my exit to exhale

The Gift

1
The gift my mother gave me,
when she threw me in that sea,
cold and deep, filled with joy
and I only a toddling boy   as if
she knew, I'd like to think,
that this was all she had to give
that this is all I have to give

2
We were young tan teens
when she wanted it, sigh,
I did not know how or why
I squinted through darkness
at faint cresting waves
listening to them peel
from a bench on the boardwalk
under a chuppah of New Jersey stars

3
For all I know and ever will
is in that certain ocean still
its depth below and waves above
the ocean, my first true love

Dad

He lie In Maimonides,
monitors beeping, a plastic tube
disappeared down his throat
like a sick magic trick I didn't get
inadequate at his feet

I should have touched him,
held his hand, kissed his brow,
offered comfort with a word, or a drug

And now, thirty years later
I feel his pain, meditating
on an uncomfortable couch
in the Highlands of Scotland
where Laury and I have been hiking
over hills, dales, glens

—

Tears wet my cheeks
damp my white beard,
my salmon eyes dripping

My Hero

I remember raking rocks out back
—maybe nine or ten at the time—
prepping our forty square-foot garden,
raking and tossing stones aside
while our funny looking dog Snoopy
played like a puppy does but
getting closer and closer to my steel rake
until I raked his foot
and got it stuck between tines
and I panicked,
the poor son of a bitch dog
is stuck in my rake
I yelled to Dad

John Wayne strolled over
placed his rake against the rusted fence,
the same fence that my friends and I
climbed on wild flings through Brooklyn's
back-alleys - escape routes from our foes—
Then dad kneeled down and
gently removed Snoopy's paw
from between the metal tines
before silently strolling back
to round up the weedy yard

Magnificent Seven

Yul Brynner was tough, and my father and I,
popcorn in our laps, together, were tough guys too
that day, that movie, before walking
Bay Parkway back home

Another day, driving with dad
in our hand-me-down ford
he screamed at other drivers "jerks"
his arms wildly waving
behind windshield and steel

..and he seemed to me to be
nothing at all like Yul Brynner

Outa Dodge

He didn't speak
you didn't stop
the door didn't slam
it might have been a
Wednesday or Saturday
when I walked down the steps
for the last time with a rucksack
filled with too many canned goods
and boots I'll soon give away
after crossing the GW bridge
with a freed convict from Georgia
seeking a new life along the Palisades

Ode to New York

O' New York, you're
so awesome when I
walk your city streets
wait for lights to change
orange letters shout DON'T WALK,
pushed on curb then off on green
Walk Walk Walk
cars fly by, eyes to ground
old lady spits, young girls whisper
freaks afraid to look

O' New York you're a
concrete jungle, sewer to sewer
a prick in a sore thumb
a pile of junk,
I'm leaving you now

Gonna drive over the GW
and leave this fuckin town
to sink into sea
with only the tip
of the Empire State Building
sticking out of the water

..and I'll paddle by to
drop pennies down the
slot on top

1960s

15

Coming Home

Traveled past where white lines end
and further still past Jersey pines
returned to pavement, streets and signs
I thought I left this past behind
slept on nails thick and thin
following your scent like a dog
jamming toe time simpleton
never been here before and
hopefully never will again

How'my gonna explain hanging out?
can I plant tulips in cement,
suck words off gabbro stones?
will the sun rise tomorrow?
there's no rush and I won't
sell nature short just don't
put me in a scissor-lock or
play stickball on my stoop

Before we go though
take the garbage out
to the alleys of 42nd street
or Ratner's, stumble into
a basement on Avenue A
to drink with musicians
we meet at a liquor store
on the first avenue we found

Reflections

I saw a murder in the mirror
while brushing my teeth
crows passing by

Today, already interesting,
like a cousins' club picnic
in Paramus, sixty years ago

Coney Island Baby

What were they thinking
that July 4th, pushing the carriage
with me on my back along the boardwalk
bustling with first and second generation
Brooklyn immigrants crowded together
like the firework finale scaring me shitless,
my fifteen-month-old when-I-do-the-math self
wailing as if loud would never end

Surprised by my earliest memory
appearing today, the canopy reeled back
the trees dancing with each breath, and the wind
the wind snaring left-over leaves and a straight-ahead sun
and cumulus clouds, high cirrus and a pomegranate sky
draped over the curvature of dismantled rollercoasters,
cotton candy and ketchup licked fingers
relishing Nathan's French fries and a coke
before laughing with kids on the N train
kicking our asses into the future

There's a Word in Yiddish

Meshugas
explains recent events
hauling, moving, boxing
meeting, accounting
meeting grandson Gus
seeing, storing, planting
mulching, mowing,
missing guitar
ferrying
to and fro
past Groton Point
flat water, Sou'west breeze
blowing so I see farther
Father now

Post for Gramps

The past got me remembering
spitting watermelon pits
off the migrant tenant's
porch steps. That dude knew how
to quarter a melon, the long way
for us kids to dive into.

Those summer days I tagged along
in hot sun with gramps
while he built houses on the farm
for seasonal farmers. We never spoke
side by side. I was useful though
and didn't know it

'get me the hammer eddie'

After Sunday dinner gramps and I
and a Mexican dog I can't spell
burned garbage in a barrel
and poked sparks into the end of day
with that snippy little dog
sitting too close to my liking
we listened to fire crackle
kicked back in aluminum watching
the rhythm of fireflies blinking
on and off into dusk before walking
back to the house at my bedtime..

..where I'd lie in bed sleepy, watching
headlights travel through the room
dreaming of nothing, waking
eager to do it all again

Here's Looking at You

..with your leather jacket draped
over your strong Riga shoulders
staring at me framed on my desk
your white hair like snow
your eyes staring at me through the lens
of your journey out of Europe to America

A minute ago I wanted more.
What ship? from where? alone?
smell? sleep? eat? money? Where
did you think you were going?

Above our home a hawk high, distant
floating then banking top branches
of spruce planted when we moved here gramps—
where we raised our children, continuing
your journey. it's so nice you visit
at times when I've not a thought
typing on a keyboard that
if it breaks you could fix
in your garage full of tools
like the acetylene torch
next to the butcher block
that you asked me to get for you
when I visited you in the hospital
and didn't recognize you, you were smaller
since last I saw you, and bars on the bed
raised because you kept trying to get home
and were willing to burn your way out
until the nurse at the desk said
if you could walk out you could go

and you did

Parents

Ms. Robin warmed her eggs
a month after Easter
on Mother's Day in Rhododendron
flowering for the forty second time
we've witnessed it flower
giving us much to think about..

By father's day pink petals
will lie upon white stones
with cracked egg then saved
to place upon a headstone
when that special day arrives

Before and after Garamond

Slim edges of letters
use less ink
than trusty old Courier
fading like Captain Columbus
sailing his ship far offshore
off to the edge of the world
like a Samurai, while Leonardo
crashed his flying machine
Jews ran, Jews ran, exiled, chased
while the Chinese brushed their teeth
with boar bristles, and Switzerland was born
while Michelangelo trimmed discarded marble
that others couldn't see was David.

1500s

The Righteous Ones

Eddie and Stevie snuck
into the sanctuary
led by the hand of g-d
to free the sacred tootsie pops
hidden under the Bema,
only let out on the Sabbath
until that day Eddie and Stevie
brought forth the pops on a weekday
unto the light of the lord

then Eddie and Stevie
—g-d bless them—
distributed the pops
to a multitude of preteens
even though they were
of low class and devious

and when all is said and done,
pages turned, Eddie and Stevie
will be inscribed in the Book of Life
for all time, for all days
and all the nights of Brooklyn
where Mouse shouldn't have ducked

Under the El in '68

1
I dreamt we were making love
in a Brooklyn apartment until
we heard steps so pulled sheets
with our feet up over our folds
then lying back you asked me
sweetly to leave

2
I walked tarred-over tracks
under the El on McDonald,
trains clackety-clack above me
heading north to Manhattan
blue tracers lit up shadows of
my childhood, alleys of my youth

I walked on, hack license in one pocket
draft card in the other, burning a hole
through my pocket, under the El
of the Independent line

Our Lady of the Harbor

I like many new Yorker's have never
visited the statue of liberty in the harbor
or been to the top of the Empire State building
or picnicked in Central Park after rowing a boat
with swans, or ice-skated in Rockefeller Center
after watching long legged Rockettes.

But you can speak with me of the Filmore East
and the friends, where one and all gathered
weekly to watch three bands for six dollars,
or speak with me of the Shah Bagh restaurant
three steps down below apartments on East 6th
where we once spent a pleasant afternoon with Henny
and the family that emigrated from Pakistan who owned it
drinking cinnamon tea spiced with hashish, communing
and sharing South Asian delicacies fulfilled into nightfall
not wanting to leave in Henny's VW van.

The gentle cook presented me with a book,
short stories he wrote for his family titled
'Letters Home'. He might've visited the statue.
Might even have felt her presence and/or his absence,
his thoughts might've wandered and wondered which.
I felt strangely effected by his gift and openness
sharing his stories with me thinking my own
goddess of liberty welcoming my ancestors.

This day a sweet offering, memories awoken.
May our Lady of the Harbor's torch remain lit
and her chains remain broken.

War

Didn't get the call
in the 60s
nor had the calling

..but gave blood
every five weeks
in New Hampshire

Walking Down 63rd

I remember Bay Parkway four-story walkup
on the corner where new tenants were hard
to find after old ones died. I played
in the coal bins with the super's kid
who's face was always smudged and bruised,
but not always from coal—
I never did think his dad was super.

Mouse lived across the street.
His mother once tried to run me down.
Mouse's dad listened to LP's in Spanish
and farted for Mouse's friends.

Leslie lived a block away in half of a whole house,
a palace, two floors, two bathrooms. I slept there
now and then. I once saw Leslie's mom washing up and his dad
on the toilet, together in the bathroom. His dad, a former boxer
was a maître d' in Manhattan. He taught Leslie to box and Leslie
taught us and hurt us. Leslie joined a neighborhood gang,
the Golden Guineas, a tough Jew with a baby face until
he went to Viet Nam. Last I heard he lived in Florida with his mom
and hung at the track, but that was a long time ago now.

Janet spun out on pills.

Howard lived on the corner.
We went through grade school together.
He's still there, walking down 63rd street
wondering where everybody went.

Trippin

That night we drove through Times Square
laughing with call girls all the way to 9th.
we didn't flinch when a dude kicked a bum
coming down from a long night tripping
you had gears on your face and
only the thousand year old pigeon
on the steps of the 42nd Street library
understood. When you moved your hands
skin slid, I wished to hell it was amusing.
Duff died with a brilliance we only glimpsed.
Myron, swept away too young.
Howie crashed into a mountainside.
Joy was not happy.
How long was the fright?

We ended that night at Nathan's in Coney Island
eating our way to Eddie's Fascination

Eddie's Table 1976 *by Linda Lou*

Thanksgiving Day
1975

Almost dinnertime,
everybody happy to see each other

Paul, in from Idaho, in the corner rolling reefer
Curt, eyeing our horses, used to ride rodeos
Little Jonathan letting loose with his 100th paper airplane
Neil, opening Champagne
Cathy, hasn't stopped talking for a minute, mistaken on
the phone for Gabby by a friend
Linda, piercing a turkey-grease blister
her face hidden in blond hair as she
inspects her injured foot
Donny, from Brooklyn, talking tough, making friends
Laury, in the fire's glow, smiling in the midst
of all the conversations

Snow falling, dogs' noses pointing toward the kitchen
YoYo, our barn cat, clinging the screen outside
hoping for sympathy from anyone to be let in
to get thrown out again
The table, my masterpiece, cut to height this morning
awaits the turkey with all the trimmings

(continued)

A line lingers by the bathroom, no rush,
the hallway smells of beer
Baby Yuda cries for a teat to suckle
Geraldine, a three-year-old artist
pastes portraits onto the refrigerator door
Judy, her mother, telling me to bring her our pheasants,
she has a wonderful recipe for pheasant
T, carrying firewood, a famous writer one day

Finally,
dinner on the table
No words of grace
just a rushed drunken pig-out
the American way

A Dale (Raoul) Rush
May 28, 1975

Sunshine morning
horses grazing
cats' asleeping
Saigon licking her morning paws
no more boys going off to war
time to get moving and soar

Summer skool is starting
I'm a student/ or a
            stewed-entity/ or a
change of papers keep the puppies clean
like a degree keeps everybody happy
but the pups wouldn't think twice
to piss on it

_____

There ain't no apocalyptic angel on my shoulders—NO
not in any of my poems. I try for a
perfect rhythm but with a fixed deck
my cards are marked with a punctured ego
looking through the eye of the Jack
that came home blinded from some big war
ain't got that peripheral vision no more
it doesn't show up in the tracks
I've marked across your floor
I mean STAE spelled backward EATS
for every buttonhole I've sewn.
if you can't smell my scent
I'll leave a shoe for you
to bang Khrushchev on your piano

(continued)

I'm behind mirrors—as if
there are more than one of me,
the other on the other side,
a koan cannot do,
if there are no sockets in the streets
to plug my soul into then I'll stay lost
in a fog that my thoughts conjure
Am I what I read in the daily paper
Did I send planes with bombs to Cambodia
Am I the one that peeled that fateful fruit
in Mexico and drove the bus off the cliff
killing all of my extensions
Am I an Arab or a Jew
Am I a fish in an ocean or a bird
in a 747 barroom, if I can't say the password
will the cave close—

      the phantom is my friend. he drove
      a big truck into a bigger tree almost
      severing his roots from this life. he
      remained locked in my cave for weeks
      then these words came and I whispered them
      and the phantom rowed his boat to shore
      and said POW, and we were saved from
      the sun that was burning our wings.

————

bird cooing on branch

    the light of day
keeps ghouls away

Dark December

Someone said writing stops time
or kills it? I'm not certain
if it's rain or snow
pattering the skylights

I'd like to fly, or cross-country ski,
blow across a frozen lake in Minerva
arms out gloved-hands spread jacket
wide like sail, wind pushing us past
Algonquin spirits in the hillside shore

Where are you Scotty, tonight, in San Francisco?
Where is Otis or Linda Lou
T or K, Bobby, Curt, Yuda, Cinders, Mariah
and Silly, where are you?

I'm here in Guilford, looking at Bro's scars,
the bite I sewed on his face from you Silly
and one on his floppy ear
but that one was another dog's doing

Four Twenty

Was listening to President Carter's energy speech
when Barbara knocked on my door to preach
Jehovah's Watchtower. I looked out at trees,
birds, bees buzzing pink flowers while she went on and on.
When I spoke she said I was over her head, me
up a step said 'Damn right'. She flipped
bible pages for quotes to appeal
I said 'I don't get g-d
didn't like him ever
since I read Exodus'.

Barbara, not swayed, sent others
but nothing is like the first time
so I plan not to be here
when they arrive, probably drive
around the neighborhood
wasting gas a different way.

Elm City Filling Stations

1
I don't have to be here,
I have choices; to stay
or follow the river
back to the ocean, or
submerge myself in petroleum

Old man Sam said
'they don't tell me nothin'
softly he spoke like
someone might hear
he said 'I had three strokes
I can't remember names
I also had a heart attack
I'm scared I'll lose my job'

2
I pushed a thief
out the car door before
he pulled a knife during
Dave Von Ronk's intermission
at the Shamrock on Chapel

3
When the sun peeks its brow
over green tanks along the Quinnipiac
I unlock gates and open valves
to let trucks in to fill
for me to pay my bills
enjoying the view but still
wondering how I got here

Russian Crude

One day
you're in North Guilford
woods all around
pumping oil at sixty five gallons per minute
filling a basement tank
and you have to shit

There are paths into these woods
beyond the house
but you can't hold on
so you ask the homeowner
to use her bathroom
smelling up her house
for eleven cents per gallon

Crazy Man

I've got to be crazy
reasoning with kids,
sounds like a song
'got to be crazy da da da da'

Thought of driving to Brooklyn today,
visit the folks in their apartment,
the one I grew up in 'till I left,
sit in the living room
—a contradiction in terms—
with nothing to say
except the kids are fine, yes, Levi is SOOOO big,
Laury is fine, yes, I would like a cup
of coffee and something to eat
then the TV magically turns on, loud

Lived that scene for five seconds
then went to Bradlees
bought a thirteen-dollar shirt
that didn't quite fit,
stopped in Radio Shack,
bought a mixer that didn't quite work,
drove to my office to write,
cursed at the cursor hanging up
called my lawyer
told him I got to be crazy

I got to be crazy
to be here with you

Love Life

Hugging by stove I rest
head upon your shoulder
spices lined up the clock ticks
4:55 rosemary, sage
cinnamon and thyme

We part stirring stew
wet sponge in hand
wipe away splatters
resume cooking dinner
resume kitchen love

I Gave it a Try

There was that time I prayed
dripping wet on a Belmar beach
exiting the ocean lost, palms together
like I knew to do from movies
to plea for help, for divine guidance
like those football players pray for
to win their games. I thought
me worthy too to find mom's chair
(what could be more important)
while she sat there watching
not fifty feet away

When I opened my eyes I saw her
staring, no wave, no bright-light,
no 'ding' of enlightenment, no
lifeguard jumping down from a chair,
no g-d that I could recognize arose
to guide me to mom's blanket.. but
only my own two feet, I came to dis-
cover that day, would ever get me
to where I need to go

Dawning

Ocean mist blankets yellow lines the
cool autumn mornings the truck pulls
right onto Old Montauk Hwy to
view the Atlantic before town,
shades of blue stretch to beach,
cars lined up in the lookout lot
strapped with boards

—where can I turn, or straighten out
like mother told me to when my
Parkway wetsuit, flung over the
outdoor shower, salted her flowers
and my bare feet traipsed sand
into our room at the Ocean Wave
across the road from the 12th street jetty
where first I found I could walk on water,
Not like Jesus, but like that's how
it's supposed to feel I've felt

Pause on a Precipice

Need to know where at,
climb a rock, cross a creek,
lean against mossy pine-bark
watch water fall off a ledge
heading to sea I guess
and knows how to get there

—breathe,

NOW more than ever—

then step off downstream
on a new trail to exhale

Better Outside

Always knew
as far back as memory,
No bad face there

Indoors lay down dizzy
lazy, rug-dirt
dust in cupboards
leaving no choice
in this clapboard home
to be anywhere but there
out by the firepit
with a white dog
grey birds perhaps
blue sky lovely
barren trees still
green grass after
muddy rain poking
fire sans guilt
of flying embers
nor shame
in all my failings

G-d

Heavy heavy word, g-d,
heaviest in the whole damn world
in all languages, billions of people
weighing it down, hell
who could blame me..

Lonely Wooden Tower

Leonard Cohen
September 21, 1934—November 7, 2016

I string guitar, tune it,
upside down and backwards
which I tend to do and
when my son brings this up
each time he plays
I tell him that's how I do
upside down and backwards

we improvise strumming along
making up songs as I strive for rights
more than wrongs, then play Leonard Cohen
tunes of festival trains and the Chelsea Hotel,
Suzanne's spice and oranges,
together by a river
—nothing rhymes with oranges—
hoping for that day
when I can stand above water
for all my children to see

ChChChanges

My next stop after dim sum
City Lights in North Beach
where I wandered lost
like many times before,
it's swell to be back
on the west coast again

I read in the I Ching
'the wise man Returneth in seven days'
after tossing three-pennies six-times
on a Colorado mountain
overlooking the Big Thompson
slicing through the canyon

east coast or west

then left for Boston the following Tuesday
in my '52 Chevy with Phil who shared an orange
and that mountaintop moment driving east
on fumes free coffee and donuts
from a Pennsylvania rest stop
keeping us safe and awake
to cross the George Washington Bridge
with Phil's lucky silver dollar to
pay the toll to cross the Hudson,
drive to a familiar house, on
a familiar block, that I thought I
left in my rearview, so many miles ago

Sunday

O' Jones:

writing this seems like a thing to do
after reading a revealing article by Patti Smith the fire
crackles damp snowed on logs. Connecticut has its share of
pollutants; snow, probably more lead than a gallon of paint.
I'm running around crazed in a three piece suit. my two-fisted
snide Brooklyn/Buffalo and all the other places these eyes
of mine have seen remarks don't quite fit the mold.
I'm impressed by Patti Smith's candor but my shades are down.
staying indoors on a sunny day messing around, reading and writing,
sipping snake-bites (Yukon Jack and lime juice) sometimes swigging
Yukon straight. if there was something else to do I might do it.
nobody's called and I don't really know anyone for miles. I guess
it's a right time for solitude. sometimes you walk around it and
other times you're in up to your neck. either way smells. maybe,
if I stayed in Brooklyn, wore a black leather jacket,
married a 'hitter', became a cop or a garbage man,
ate at Tang Fong's every Sunday night..

> Then I thought of Robert Frost
> in New England and asked him
> which road to take, he said
> it doesn't much matter
> just keep moving forward
> to all four corners
> if need be

ed

You Could have been There

The argument went on
what seemed forever,
toothpicks; wood vs. plastic.
it was Jim's idea to cross the sandbar
at hightide to the island
moving slow the sun done rising
Sunday, drinking all day

Never made it to the island
splashed until we tired
cold and wet

but

I really can't remember
maybe Jim does

Sixty's Sonata Knell

Light shows, dayglo, be-ins
sit-ins, yippies and peace signs, Manson
and Altamont, D.C. tear gas burnt eyes,
blood in streets in the jungle in Dallas convertible
on Memphis terrace in a Lost Angel's kitchen
and stage in the Heights..

while hippies played with flowers
in hair at Monterey Pop

..and Kerouac sang with Steve Allen's piano
'I'd rather be thin than famous'
before drinking himself to death

Indian Lake Story Regarding Abundance

Moving our stuff from
van into house back
to van back to house
moving, this time to corn-patch land by a lake

On one trip to the van I noticed brush
towards the tracks near the dirt road, burning.
Being from Brooklyn, a place you're born
to not get involved
I stay myself
and watch the fire spread,
brush and weeds and little trees.

Carrying our old Zenith into our lake house
I stopped to rest and watch the flames
wondering if everybody in Michigan
burn garbage this way. Gnats swarmed
around my sweaty head in my eyes as
I rise to pick up a lamp and two suitcases
as our new neighbor hurried past. Hello I say
smiling, pointing to the flames
closing in on his house.
He grabbed a hose and shouted for his son
who burst from the garage prepared with shovels
running toward the fire like it wasn't his
first time. I helped by pouring water,
out of YoYo's litter box, without exchanging names.

(continued)

I walked back to the van with knees bent,
lifted a heavy box of records, the van
finally empty. I was glad the fire was out.
I hated like hell to have to move again.

August 1976

Business School

1
This year I'm
acutely aware of spring fever
back in school in Michigan
two birds dance rebirth
on a limb out the window,
Petroleum 432, distributive education
one bird walks
the other's head nods
then walks kinda hops too

2
We're in this together,
my fellow students
the birds and I,
hopping and bopping into the future

1976

Grad School

1
This year I'm
acutely aware of my sever-
ley inflicted Spring fever

two birds dance rebirth outside
petroleum 432, distributive education
one walks the other watches
then walks kinda hops too

2
New born buds on bushes—
how did a bud get its name
Bud—do birds sing
a poet's lament
'O Bud'

3
We'll fly home
after graduation
and put these birds to use

Embers

I sat at the table in the seventies
with Richard Raymond, Rebecca Newth-Harrison,
Katrina, Gwen, Pat, Dee Dee, Karen, and
Margaret Deal Wilson, who with her husband
sailed up the Connecticut River as far as they could
from New Orleans many years before, and shared
her dream-laden poems full of lush beauty
like the salt marsh in Chester that wooed her.

Gordy stopped by this morning with a smile
and an anthology of poems. Gordy poet/realtor
found us this home in 1981. Cold air swept past me
at the open door where I didn't know what to say
but thanks then went back inside to sit by fire
and read poems of flowers and birds I did not know.

I was tuning my guitar when Gordy rang the bell,
resuming when he left, playing Leonard Cohen
songs about the Chelsea Hotel, Suzanne, her spices
and oranges down by the river—
then I read poems in the present pleasantly
surprised to recognize white herons in Salt Marsh,
rocks lining the West River channel, ospreys,
and voracious cormorants eating fish, depleting
the food chain, forcing large fish out to sea.
I also, happily, noticed a lack of punctuation
next to the fireplace in the glow of embers.

Pea Soup Fog,

for Vessel Riga, a Good ol' Boat

Words failed this morning,
this page a ghostly anchor
holding back a winding river
morning-fog dinghy ride
to Riga to start engine,
the gut at slack awaits no one

Stowing fresh water and pretzels
for a twenty mile run
the fog lifted so fell behind a boat
in river tween rock breakwaters
the engine quit at the mouth
so unfurled jib in five knot winds
barely reaching clear water

A long long day in little breeze
without sight of course no power for
ten hours moored hot and hungry
with no inclination to tidy lines till the morrow,
maybe write about the fog, how it felt all over again

Chappy

Can't remember the end of my dream
there were kids and dogs running,
no sharks or upset boats,
while swaying on anchor to wind

I'd rather of dreamt of just one
good idea drinking morning coffee
in dew covered cockpit
gazing up river to Essex

Another Birthday, March 24ᵗʰ 2017

This one is different
which you would think it would be just
another day similar to yesterday
and forty two days before, that day
bumped and bruised knocked out on the rug
before EMT's lifted painfully, and I'm hearing
from friends on two legs who can smell roses
or why bother living while I'm laid up
lying down, a refrigerator chilling
my fucked up leg.

I'm thinking of sweets watching my NCAA bracket
take a pathetic turn and learning more than
I ever needed to about Verne, the voice of the Southern
Conference for the last seventeen years. Everyone loves
Verne. He met his wife of 45 years through classical
music, not basketball. Why should you care? Why do I?
I just want to see a player run and stay airborne, aloft,
weave a ball through a hoop.

No cake or balloons this year, nuh-uh,
not like those years clothespin clipping
cards in spokes cutting up alleys flicking
them cards and punching balls in narrow
space between walls I now can touch with
arms spread if I could stand. A new wave
of immigrant mothers push strollers on our street
but are unable to see their kids futures
in our spotted faces.

I, for sure, never saw it coming.

We city slingers sprung over fences
like pogos, ducking and bobbing
at crossroads, learning the ropes
that got us through unscathed
fortunate to arrive, scars and all.

Mr Wiggles just wanna Dance

Happiest fella you ever did see
smiling bug-eyed tall and blown-up crazy
arms waving with tireless wind
he feels the beat and dances all day
next to racks of tires he doesn't understand
how they sit so still he's having a ball
kids love him, wave and yell out 'hi'
from back seats cruising by

But at night, when traffic abates
his fun ends and he bends in half
just about kissing the dirty curb
bereft and deflated, all that remains
of the day is jealousy of his Tall Boy buddy
who's got the fast food gig next door
dancing all day and all through the night
while he can't bathed in sad moonlight
looking like Bazooka Joe standing
lit by the light of a light pole
searching for something he lost
a long long time ago

Grown Up

Pouring scotch
into afternoon coffee

the bird
that was
in the garage
three days
died
I think it was
mother

I offered seeds
water, an opposable thumb
to gently lift her hollow bones
into air for one last flight
before placing her by
the edge of the woods

The Peterson Guide
useless, a relic, useless
as I, copyright 1950

New Day

1
Rain's done,
jungle's softer,
typical Costa Rican music
floats over the hedgerow
mixed with birds whistling
and waves pounding Suck Rock,
and barking

birds take flight
in this new world

2
I re-connected
during the downpour
with friends from the hood

we're planning to fly again too

to float the Colorado
before the sun sets
on this wily jungle adventure

Grand Canyon

Can't find the words
to describe
how life changed
in the month of May 2011
after sixty one years on this planet

What words can describe
a six-million year-old canyon

pristine? majestic? spiritual magic?

I can see John Wesley Powell
one hundred fifty years ago
paddling a wooden boat
with only one arm and
and two very large balls
while duck-diving a wave
in a rubber raft
full of friends

Sunday in Sonoma

Tossing balls
over emptied glasses
grins decanted, all net

We're slouched in wicker
in this home above birds,
webbed in magic spells, basking
in our lengthened shadows

while rain falls, and the dog sleeps

After Jazz Fest

I missed my connection in D.C. by minutes
but that was all that was needed
to sit in Ronald Reagan airport for hours

Last night Steve and I enjoyed a
concert for Obama in NOLA that rocked,
another late-night groove of music and food
Danielson texting us not to come home.

- Chicory coffee, beignets, Jack Daniels,
green apples, berries and oatmeal,
chocolate covered ginger, coconut
paddies, red beans and rice..

and yoga after breakfast
before hitting funky streets
to never return the same
as if only we had a chance to

Cats at the Katzs'

1
Florida
freakin Florida
at Bobby's house
in Fort Lauderdale,
cats everywhere

on the bed, under it
in the closet and left-open drawers
herded by Iggy
their vigilant sheep dog

I have no use for these felines
never have except once
as a mouser for a Buffalo barn

2
Gregory Corso was right,
his whiskey heart full
of sad cat paintings, his
sad life of cats hanging

3
Next time we travel
we'll stay in a hotel
like normal people
on vacation

The Road,
for Kenny

It ain't no use man
the games played out, the
pretzels are stale, eaten,
digested, gone

    If the buildings were all blown,
        swept away, trees planted,
        maybe then I'd return
        set up camp and sing around a fire
        passing bottles roasting mellows
        but until that time all I can do
        is hope the island doesn't sink
        till my friends are safe on shore
        for never lasts what was before

Begin Again

Should I be sad
or happy for him
leaving home

the car full
my heart perplexed
my brain befuddled

This is What I do

Trees trees trees in these woods
the dog sniffing end of day coffee
smelling of peaty scotch with
just-out-of-the-oven sourdough bread
the dog is gnawing the chewy crust

These trees are falling apart
into gutters accepting winter's
slanted sun illuminated moldy roof,
rotting deck, a window to replace
like knees this road wore down
and sore back of years cutting
splitting and stacking
so not to topple

—

Hobbling and cobbling through time
an old rocker on an uneven porch
or the hanging chair in Amagansett, empty
but still dangling for sake of this

Shorts

Walked into wind
Monday rained into Tuesday
It was unexpected

Sounds like a train
On its way to Wednesday
Stopped to listen

This afternoon full of sun
Slanted on the
backside of waves

You don't need to feel pretty
To cook dinner
The evening arrives casually

On the sideline
For the day
To end

Lock all doors
It's bedtime
The moon just topped a tupelo

Come

There's nowhere to get
no further to go, no scroll
of instructions to begin
let alone hang hopes on

—dig the hole deep
fill it to brim
with our cat and dogs
then cover the grave
with Seneca stones
to keep animal spirits
alive forever and ever—

And you can visit anytime
        I wish you would
with your outstretched arms
place pretty flowers on
their wooded rocky tombs

A Sunday Late June

We've been on this Island awhile
clearing wintered leaves, planted a garden
salted in ocean mist hanging the hammock
and a chair pruned with music
clearing bird nests from porch rafters
in afternoon shade a momma bird
builds her nest above the high-speed fan

It's complete,
chicks chirp
floating in my nest
the dog on her bed
wet, sniffing

Napeague Overflowing

Fog rolls over the dunes
muting harbor views leaving
half a cell tower in mist, and
we, the dog and I, sit on a grey log
that I've sat on with another dog
when the same tower touched blue sky

Eel grass cowlicks brushed by waves
pop along gone glaciers' sandy shoulders
walked upon while the dog salivates past dinner
digging headlong into dusk, over the brim
toward a sturgeon moon hiding behind fog
—an earned respite I suppose
from last night's fabulous shining

Moving On

as one does
passing days with the life of a dog

you love

watching an Osprey feed her babes
peddling along Cranberry Hole

Eyeglass

I
If my eyes give out
when I'm older
my glass will be filled

II
Contact lenses
a possibility but
I can't see inserting
energy into this

III
The flower in sight
will soon be mowed dandelion

Sonoma Meditation

Breathe
Remember
Breathe
Your children will replace you
Breathe
Swaddle you
Breathe
Float you down river
Breathe

Eastwoods

Walked this Autumn morning
surrounded by oaks
and moss

no mushrooms growing
on this ol stump

Marigny

"There's nothing dudes"
I say to small birds
joining me cooing
while I sip coffee
poking a muffin

Pigeons appear
they coo too
all of us together in the Marigny
at, around, and on a round metal table, posing
as a guy across Bourbon
is getting pulled by a big dog
following his nose

We, the birds and I, watch
knowing we'll all get there
but not yet, coffee's hot and tasty
muffin crumbs with friends

Walking Down Whitfield

Walking down Whitfield
to sell my gold tooth
for thirty-two dollars

   wishing I had more

Karma

No one knew our buddha,
stolen with a scarf around his neck,
was so heavy it took five suffering men
to know him to carry the weight of the world
on their young meager thieving shoulders

Mid December in Vermont

Sun painted spruce
pricked my eyes today
the dog needs picking up
now that her muscles are big
she's shopping again

—sun reflecting off
fresh beautiful morning snow
dazzles through the boughs

An Outside Beginning

The moon on one side
pink sky on the other
dusk, chilled, alone
thinking this way about time
how our sown seeds have seeds of their own
—missing dear young ones—

Perennial lists grow unprepared
circling the drain uncompromised
making no sense, then the poor poker
tipped over, its luck run out
and it doesn't matter ruminating
in the bed of the can't-sleep-for-trying
waiting for day to break, get back to
begin again, pick up the poker and poke

CSI Eastwoods

I'm hiking a red trail
the same trail hiked two days ago
now ice covered
so I keep to edges on corn snow
careful as a night crawler
studying each step
I spy leaves, rocks, boot prints

Are they mine from the other day?
I place my foot alongside one
it's different
like snowflakes
I float by

Whose prints then
if not mine
as I turn onto today's
taking me home to write up
this days investigation

Downtown Sonoma

I'm not sure,
does deficit of attention
encourage one to wander
as well, can wisdom
arrive if idle

Sitting on a wall sur-
rounding a Spanish Mission
a stretch away from natives
etched in bronze, I feel
past beneath my feet

A good thing?
red dirt in my soles I sift
through sunsets of my youth
from a certain piece of Brooklyn
of my own graves end

CVS Pickup

Today is the first day of Spring
it's snowing again on the CVS drive-through line,
white flakes like floaters, Spring not yet sprung
another day in New England
and at the window I forget
to place a hat on my head
depressing the button for drugs

Numbers Letters Numbers

1   F
2   U
3   C
4   N
5   N Y 6 7

Fence Posts

No good can come

With 'you look like..'

Or, 'you should..'

I'm napping

Summertime

They came before they left
hydrangeas blooming
when storm clouds lifted
the beach thinking
where did they go
those whales where
and kids too go for only
into the well of memory

Where did they go,
smudged chalk still on the door,
on the walk, a single flipper
underwater, the last puzzle piece
spinning in the spa, the porch empty
quiet, dredging a hole into this
picture puzzle called life
simmering and shimmering to behold

Thanksgiving 2019

Missed poetry today
The plane left
My son still in Chicago

Drizzling

A soaked fallen beech
softens leaves beneath
—mushrooms blossoming

This performance
is not a rehearsal
nor practice,
the sky decomposing,
intelligent, gray

Birthday Poem March 2021

Barely made another trip around the sun
behind a pallet of grey in the face of trees

   wish their limbs could embrace us

They say it'll be alright, we'll
take care of everything, relax, you
made it, it's your birthday, Halleluiah

Ripple

Waves of sense
wash over surfers
sliding towards shore
then receding beside jetty
to sea again float
in red hues of sky
glassing off evening
our hearts unstrung

Rainy Night in Guilford

Suitcase open on the bed
caught me cold thinking
about traveling west while
rain's still falling you said
you called it and all I could do
was wander to my desk in agreement

In the beginning morning woke grey
before rain beat me into woods with dog
rain soaked in pattered hood. Fallen
limbs and broken trees scattered
about like last night's dreams that
I can't quite make out why
this hike seems familiar so back to
home again where skylights tell of weather
and the dog spins to curl by the fire
'Toss the suitcase out the window
I don't need it anymore' Dylan laments
caged in anigre cabinet speakers
while I lie next to the dog
sinking into rug with fire and rain
to absorb the night seeping
into my resting bones content
with my lot in life this whole damp day

We the People Wish a New Year

We the people wish peace,
hope peace, that's all

We the people; freedom
for us and all others

We the people are tired of bullets

We the people wish healthcare, and choices
and art, and education without religion
not bullets, bullets, and more fucking bullets
due to a fuckin comma—

We the people..

We the people wish earth be The priority
for all else pales and will be forgotten

..and we the people wish a plague of locusts
on congress on that field of pandering nitwits

..and we the people wish the sea to part
and all but chariots make it to heaven

..and we the people wish everyone
a happy and healthy new year

Green Hat

The army-green sunhat fit,
a drawstring for wind,
cost eighty five dollars, my g-d
or whomever stopped me
from replacing my twelve-dollar
ragged straw hat purchased last
year at the IGA

Am I thinking clearly
or just sorting and shifting
like shore break sand
looking for a better break
down the road that's waiting
as long as it takes to get there

Growing by Half

1
Sitting in beach chairs
a dear friend and I stare
at forever sea talking
like two fellows do
about this and that
sail drawing wind, a barge
heading west, no whales today,
nice waves though, reckoning
it takes a lifetime to comprehend
the ins and outs of a red streaked sky
coloring those streets and alleys
we once ran thru, now invisible, like
the sandy dunes we climbed to get here

2
At a certain age
you can count again
in half years,
you can choose
which crack to step on,
to eat greens or not
wear a tie, you get
to choose which
trail to sidestep
or step in, who
to believe and when
to leave..

    plenty of time
is a question, celebrate
that not too distant place
where we become one
with worms and reputation
good or bad celebrate
missing nothing and everything
like the majestic stand of trees
this sunset pours through, for us,
before darkness drinks their crowns

Astral

I look up to see sound piercing clouds
The Japanese maple fed too much died
Learning how little we need

Tomorrow isn't promised
they say but stars always
after we are after they
are a memory

A conundrum,
when I pass
know me by actions
before bursting into flames
streaking across a night sky
for your eyes only

Bandit,

for a guy and a small dog I knew

He's gone to a place where all dogs go
packed with the good ones
ones that love and were loved
the ones that loved you down to bone

That sad day
he ran through your heart
stealing peace, just before
the screen door slammed

Snow in Ukraine

The sun sets, and sets

and might rise again

but for fewer

at both ends of the shovels

Art Upon his Passing

On Chaffinch Island Road
where white heron and ospreys soar over salt marsh
lived a gentle man who always smiled
with only pizza and bottles of coke in his frig
and a single tray of cubes in the icebox..

When we moved the living room table
it revealed his tan carpet
was originally blue

How could this happen
to our gentle friend
who was kind and always smiled

and was such a
good card player

Scotty Rest in Peace
Feb 25, 1949 – May 10, 2023

Chuck called from California with the news
turning this beautiful New England Spring morning
heavy. With Dark Star floating through speakers
tears wet my cheeks picturing you Scotty
with a Lark cigarette between your fingers
on our farm in Williamsville, head tilted, hair
flowing in the orchard across your atavistic face
looking like you're about to say something that you will not say
and I too for once have no words, just so many memories
flooding forth through this broken earthen dam of life today
where men and women our age are dying too damn young
where death don't have no mercy in this land

Thanksgiving 2023

Another trip around the sun
kids arrived and the dog was happy,
more to love she jumps

I'm eating vegan leftovers
and have the honor to mutilate the turkey
to display on a plate I don't mind

Gus built a world in the study
Levi stayed home a bit
longer than planned
Kate's back on the island
already missing all the fun

Styrofoam Dancer

I drove by a woman dancing with hands
leading arms of a snowman wearing a top hat
high stepping scrub and brush
on the edge of holding on through winter

This pandemic's twisting everyone silly
like that dancing woman flailing
with abandon and pleasure shouting
we're not All dead, not yet
any way I'd rather be dancing too,
not driving by, dancing with whomever
in a crowd of happy people like
in Netflix movies we're consuming,
like the snowman with the top hat
and the lady along the way
dancing cheek to cheek, cheek
to everlasting cheek

Not Yet

This is not that day,
not yet, summer hanging on,
hydrangeas big, rusty,
round a month before leaves drop
that we won't miss
if today were then

   we become this day
    this day becomes
old bones aching with each footfall
a particular reward for today's waking
and I think it was Roshi who said
'suffering is your paradise'
and maybe he was right but
not quite the right answer one wants
in this field of possibilities
where but for the days darken earlier
and the trail ahead winds quicker to the sea
where it all began where sunsets light the path
and stars twinkle a map in the sky
to follow to forever

Why Bother

All poetry's been written it's said
blue marble clouds move past this
rock next to my chair beneath black cherry
and a shadow of hawk appears before hawk
a red winged blackbird calls, calling attention,
tree tops sway and a lit disc behind moving clouds
bursts into blue before eyes in the distance
the deer and her doe twitching
this forest of scattered poems
entangled in wineberry

The Author

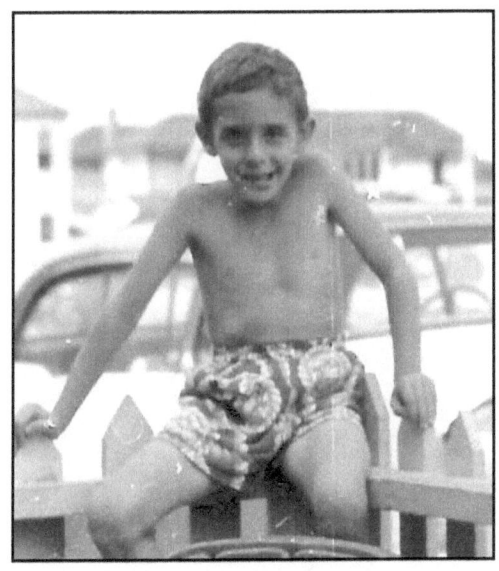

Rockaway Beach 1950s

www.ingramcontent.com/pod-product-compliance
Lightning Source LLC
Chambersburg PA
CBHW020417130626
46549CB00006B/2599